Dreams with Meaning

Adrian Collins

Adrian Collins

Adrian Collins

First edition
All Rights Reserved
Author: © Adrian Collins

Reproduction of this book in whole or in part, or its transmission by any means, is prohibited without the express written permission of the author. Any unauthorized use constitutes an infringement of copyright.

Copyright holder: © Julian Velandia

Index

Introduction to Dreams

Dreams have fascinated mankind since time immemorial. Throughout history, people have tried to understand why we dream and what those strange images that appear while we sleep mean. Since ancient civilizations, dreams have been considered divine messages, predictions of the future, or even connections to the spiritual world. The Egyptians, for example, believed that dreams were a window into the minds of the gods, and the Greeks thought that dreams could reveal deep truths about life. But what are dreams really, and why do we have them?

When we sleep, our brain doesn't shut down completely, but continues to work, organizing memories, processing emotions and, in a way, creating little stories that come in the form of dreams. These dreams can seem totally absurd, like flying over a city or talking to animals, but they can also reflect things we've experienced, like a conversation we had the day before or a situation that worries us. The interesting thing about dreams is that they don't always make logical sense; it's as if the brain allows itself to play with reality, mixing known elements with things that seem taken from a fantasy world.

It's funny to think that we all dream, even if we don't always remember it. Some studies show that we all have between three and six dreams a night, but many of those dreams are forgotten as soon as we wake up. Scientists believe that dreaming is a natural part of the sleep process, and that it somehow helps the brain organize the information it has collected during the day. Although it's not known for sure why we dream, some believe that dreams serve an important purpose: helping us process emotions, solve problems, or even prepare us for difficult situations.

Dreams can also be very varied. Sometimes we dream about people we know, other times about places we have never seen. Some dreams can be so real that, when we wake up, we have a hard time telling whether what we have dreamed really happened or not. There are also lucid dreams, those in which we are aware that we are dreaming and we can even try to control what happens. It is a fascinating experience, since at that moment we feel like the directors of our own film.

In everyday life, it is common for dreams to be interpreted in different ways. Many people believe that dreams are important messages that try to tell us something about our lives. For example, if you dream that you are losing something, some think that this may mean that you are afraid of losing something important in real life, such as a relationship or an opportunity. Others believe that dreams are simply the result of what goes through our minds before we sleep, and that they do not have a deep meaning. However, for many, dreams are a valuable tool to understand what is happening in their emotional and psychological life.

Over time, different theories about dreams have emerged to try to explain their purpose. Sigmund Freud, a famous psychologist, believed that dreams were the way to the unconscious, that part of our mind that holds desires and thoughts that we are not always willing to acknowledge. For him, dreams were like a kind of puzzle that, if we manage to decipher, could reveal very important things about ourselves. Carl Jung, another important psychologist, thought that dreams were full of symbols and archetypes that connected with the deepest part of the human being, with universal ideas that we all share. In any case, dreams remain a mystery in many ways, but at the same time they offer us a unique window to explore our minds.

Despite all that has been studied about dreams, there is still much to discover. Every night when we fall asleep, we enter a new world, full of possibilities and mysteries. Dreams can be a powerful tool to get to know ourselves better and to face life's challenges from a new perspective. Maybe the next time you wake up after a strange or fascinating dream, you will stop to think about what your mind is trying to tell you. Perhaps there, in those dreams that seem so far away and yet so close, lies a small clue about who you are and where you are going.

The Science of Dreaming

The act of dreaming is something we all experience, but have you ever wondered what happens in our brains while we sleep? The science of dreaming is a fascinating field that helps us understand how and why our dreams take shape while we rest. Although the content of dreams may seem like a mystery, what happens in our brains during sleep follows fairly clear patterns that scientists have studied for years.

It all starts with the sleep cycle, which is divided into several stages. When we lie down and relax, our body begins to go through different phases of sleep that repeat themselves several times throughout the night. These phases include light sleep, deep sleep, and the REM phase, which is when most dreaming occurs. REM stands for "rapid eye movement," and during this phase, our eyes move rapidly under our eyelids, as if we were looking at something, even though we are actually asleep.

The interesting thing about REM sleep is that the brain is very active, almost as active as when we are awake. During this phase, the areas of the brain related to emotions, memories, and imagination are particularly active. This is why dreams can be so vivid and emotional, and often seem to have connections to things we are worried about or have been thinking about during the day. At the same time, other parts of the brain, such as those that control logic and reasoning, are much less active. This explains why dreams sometimes make no sense, because the brain is creating stories without the rules of logic that we normally follow when we are awake.

One of the big questions scientists have been asking is why we dream. Although there is no definitive answer, there are several theories. One of the most popular is that dreaming helps our brains process the information and memories we accumulate during the day. While we sleep, the brain organizes and saves important memories, and some experts believe that dreams are a kind of "byproduct" of that process. It's as if the brain is reviewing what we've experienced, and as it does so, it creates scenes and situations that we later see as dreams.

Another theory suggests that dreams help us deal with our emotions. Sometimes, when we are very stressed or have a lot on our minds, our dreams reflect those feelings. For example, it is common to have anxiety dreams before an important exam or when we are facing a big challenge in life. Some studies have even shown that dreaming can help us deal with fears or emotional problems, as it allows us to experience difficult situations in a safe environment, inside our minds.

But not everything in the world of dreams is emotion or memory. There is also evidence that dreaming plays an important role in creativity. During REM sleep, the brain combines ideas in ways it normally wouldn't when we're awake. This can lead to creative solutions to problems or even new ideas we wouldn't have considered otherwise. In fact, many famous people, such as inventors and artists, have said that some of their best ideas came from a dream. It's as if the brain, while we're dreaming, allows itself to experiment without the restrictions of real life, giving us the chance to see things from a completely new angle.

In addition to the REM phase, other parts of the sleep cycle are also important. During the deeper phases of sleep, when we are not dreaming, our body and brain restore and regain energy. This rest is essential for our physical and mental health. Without it, we would not be able to function properly during the day. Deep sleep is like a kind of "maintenance" for our body, while REM sleep, where dreaming occurs, could be seen as a space where the brain explores, processes and creates.

Interestingly, it's not just humans who dream. Many animals, such as dogs and cats, also go through REM phases and are believed to dream. If you've ever seen a dog moving its legs while sleeping, it may be dreaming about running or playing. This suggests that the process of dreaming is fundamental to many living beings, not just humans.

Although we have made great strides in understanding what happens in the brain during sleep, there is still much we don't know. The science of dreaming is still a constantly developing field, and every year more is discovered about how our brains work while we sleep. What is clear is that dreams are an essential part of our lives, not only because they allow us to explore fantastic worlds or relive experiences, but because they play a crucial role in how we process what happens to us and how we deal with our emotions.

In short, dreaming is a fascinating and complex function of the brain. Although we don't always understand why we dream what we dream, we do know that this process is related to the way we store memories, manage emotions, and find new ideas. Every night, when we close our eyes, our brains are still working, connecting ideas, solving problems, and exploring corners of our minds that we may not be aware of. Dreaming is more than just a series of images; it's a window into what's going on inside us while we rest.

An Overview

Dreams are a common experience that we all share, but what many don't know is that there are different types of dreams, and each one can have unique characteristics. Throughout our lives, we've probably experienced several types of dreams without realizing that there's a pattern behind them. Some dreams fill us with joy, others leave us confused, and some can be downright scary. In this chapter, we'll take a tour of the different types of dreams, so you can better understand what's happening when your mind dives into the dream world.

One of the most well-known types of dreams is lucid dreaming. These are dreams where you suddenly realize that you are dreaming. It can be an amazing experience because when you realize that you are in a dream, you can often take control of what happens. Imagine being able to fly, visit fantastical places, or even change the ending of a nightmare. Lucid dreaming is a kind of "superpower" that some people have learned to develop. Not everyone experiences these types of dreams on a regular basis, but there are techniques that can help you have more of them if you are interested in exploring them.

Another type of dream that many people experience is recurring dreams. These are dreams that repeat over and over again, with little variation. Sometimes, you may dream about the same situation, place, or even the same people. Recurring dreams are often linked to unresolved emotional or psychological situations. For example, if you repeatedly dream that you are facing a dangerous or stressful situation, your mind may be trying to tell you that there is something in your real life that you need to resolve. Although these dreams can be upsetting, they are also an opportunity to pay attention to what your subconscious is trying to tell you.

Nightmares are another type of dream that we've all probably experienced at some point. Nightmares are often scary or disturbing, and they leave us with an unpleasant feeling when we wake up. They can be triggered by stress, anxiety, or even something we've seen or experienced during the day. Children tend to have more nightmares than adults, but anyone can have one from time to time. Nightmares, while uncomfortable, can also be a way to release repressed fears and emotions. Like recurring dreams, they sometimes show us things we need to process, but in a more dramatic way.

On the other hand, there are also vivid dreams, which are those that feel extremely real. During a vivid dream, the details are so clear and sharp that when you wake up, it can be difficult to tell whether it was a dream or something that actually happened. These dreams can be filled with colors, sounds, and sensations that seem very authentic. Some people report that after a vivid dream they can remember even the smallest details, such as the facial expressions of the people in the dream or the smell of the place they were in. Although they don't always have a deep meaning, vivid dreams are often related to times when we are more emotionally charged or stressed.

One type of dream that has generated a lot of curiosity throughout history is precognitive dreams. These are dreams in which you seem to predict something that is going to happen in the future. Although there is no scientific proof that these dreams can actually predict the future, many people have claimed to have these types of experiences. It is possible that we simply remember dreams that coincide with future events and forget those that do not come to pass. However, precognitive dreams remain a topic of interest as they raise questions about the connection between our subconscious and what happens in real life.

There are also prophetic or spiritual dreams, which many people interpret as messages from something larger or divine. Throughout history, many religions and cultures have believed that gods or spiritual beings could communicate through dreams. These dreams often have strong symbolism or a sense of transcendence that leaves a strong impression on the person experiencing them. Although not everyone believes in these types of dreams, they remain an important part of the human experience and have influenced decisions, beliefs, and even entire cultural movements.

We cannot forget to mention problem-solving dreams, those in which our mind seems to work while we sleep to find a solution to something that is troubling us. There are many stories of inventors, artists and scientists who have found solutions to complex problems or had creative ideas while asleep. During sleep, the brain continues to work, and sometimes, without interference from our conscious thoughts, it finds answers that we had not considered before. These dreams can be really helpful, especially if we are dealing with a dilemma or making an important decision.

Finally, there are fantasy dreams, those that seem straight out of a fairy tale. In these types of dreams, we can fly, visit magical worlds, or have supernatural powers. These are dreams that allow us to escape from reality and explore possibilities that do not exist in our everyday lives. These dreams, although they often seem irrelevant or simply entertaining, can also be related to our deepest desires or the need to free ourselves from the limitations of the real world.

Each type of dream offers a new way to explore our mind and emotions. Through them, we can better understand what worries us, what we desire, and what we need to resolve in our lives. Dreams, in all their forms, are a valuable tool for self-exploration and self-knowledge. Although they may sometimes seem disconcerting or even disturbing, every dream has something to tell us if we are willing to listen. The next time you close your eyes and enter the world of dreams, perhaps you can begin to notice what type of dream you are experiencing and what it might be trying to reveal to you.

The Unconscious in Dreams

The unconscious is a mysterious part of our mind that, although we don't always notice it, plays a very important role in our thoughts, emotions and behaviors. It's like a big warehouse where all those memories, desires and fears that we're not always aware of having are kept. And one of the moments when the unconscious expresses itself most freely is while we're dreaming. When we sleep, our conscious mind shuts off and makes room for the unconscious to take over, creating the dreams we experience every night.

Psychologist Sigmund Freud was one of the first to talk about the unconscious in dreams. For him, dreams were a direct window into that part of our mind that normally remains hidden. Freud believed that our dreams were a kind of coded message from the unconscious, full of hidden symbols and meanings. According to his theory, dreams reveal the desires that we don't always allow ourselves to have when we're awake, especially those that we repress because they don't fit with what we consider appropriate or right. Thus, dreams become a way to release those internal tensions without the restrictions of logic or social norms.

To better understand how the unconscious works in dreams, we can think of common examples. Imagine that you dream that you are walking through a dark forest and suddenly you get lost. At first glance, it may seem like just a random and meaningless situation, but from the perspective of the unconscious, that forest can represent an aspect of your life in which you feel lost or confused. The fact that you are lost in the dream can be a manifestation of some insecurity or doubt that you are experiencing in your daily life, something that you may not have wanted to consciously face. The unconscious takes that emotion and transforms it into an image or story that presents itself during the dream.

Another example could be dreaming about flying. Many people have had this type of dream in which they can suddenly rise into the air and feel incredible freedom. This type of dream can be related to the desire to free oneself from a difficult situation or the need to overcome obstacles. In this case, the unconscious uses flying as a metaphor for that feeling of wanting to escape or overcome something that is happening in real life. Thus, what seems to be a fantastic or fun dream can have a deeper meaning when we analyze it from the perspective of the unconscious.

The unconscious can also reveal itself through the symbols that appear in dreams. Often, the objects or people we see in dreams are not what they seem at first glance. For example, dreaming about a house can symbolize the person themselves, with each room representing different aspects of our life or our mind. If a room in the dream is messy, it could be a sign that there is something in your life that needs to be organized or resolved. These symbols are not always universal; each person has their own set of experiences and associations that influence the meaning of dreams. What for one person may be a symbol of peace, for another may represent conflict or fear.

Carl Jung, another important psychologist, had a different view of the unconscious in dreams. For Jung, dreams were not only a way of expressing repressed desires, as Freud believed, but were also a way of connecting with the "collective unconscious." This term refers to the idea that all humans share certain universal symbols and archetypes in their dreams. Jung believed that through dreams, we access these universal images that are deeply rooted in the human psyche. Thus, dreaming about a hero, a mother, or a journey, for example, could be a manifestation of these archetypes that are part of the common human experience.

The unconscious can also help us solve problems through dreams. Sometimes when we are too focused on something during the day, we can block our ability to find solutions. But when we sleep, the unconscious continues to work on the problem without the barriers we put up when we are awake. That is why many people have said that they found the answer to a dilemma or a new approach to a project after dreaming about it. The unconscious is capable of seeing things from different angles, and dreams offer us a creative way of thinking that is not always available in our daily lives.

Furthermore, the unconscious in dreams not only reflects what is happening in the present, but can also be linked to past experiences. Sometimes, dreams bring back memories from our childhood or moments that we have forgotten, but which still have an impact on how we feel or act today. The unconscious can bring up these memories to help us process or understand them better. Sometimes, these memories appear in disguised form in dreams, and it is only when we analyze them that we can understand what they are really trying to communicate.

An interesting thing about the unconscious is that it doesn't follow the rules of logic or time. In dreams, events can happen in an illogical order, people we haven't seen in years can suddenly appear, or we can jump from one place to another without any explanation. This happens because the unconscious isn't limited by the same structures as our conscious mind. In this way, dreams allow us to experience a freedom that we don't always have in real life, as the unconscious doesn't concern itself with what's possible or impossible.

Ultimately, the unconscious in dreams is a source of inner wisdom that, while we may not always understand it at first glance, has much to tell us. Through dreams, the unconscious speaks to us in a symbolic language that, if we learn to interpret, can offer us valuable clues about our deepest emotions, desires, and fears. Dreams offer us the opportunity to explore parts of ourselves that are not always in plain sight, and by paying attention to what they are telling us, we can learn a lot about who we really are.

The next time you have a dream, think about what part of your unconscious might be trying to communicate with you. Maybe there is something that your conscious mind has ignored, but your unconscious wants you to pay attention to. Dreams are, in many ways, a bridge between our conscious and unconscious minds, and through them we can discover an inner world full of meaning and possibilities.

Symbolic Interpretation

Symbolic dream interpretation is one of the most powerful tools for making sense of what our minds are showing us while we sleep. Often, when we wake up after having a dream, we are left thinking about what we just experienced: Why did I dream about a giant dog? Why did I see myself walking in an unfamiliar city? These questions arise because dreams do not usually communicate directly, but rather use symbols to convey messages. Understanding these symbols allows us to decipher what the dream is really trying to tell us.

When we talk about symbols in dreams, we are referring to images, objects, or situations that represent something deeper. For example, dreaming about water can have several meanings depending on the context. Water is often associated with emotions, as it is fluid and changing, just like our feelings. If the water in the dream is calm, it could represent inner peace or a stage of tranquility in your life. On the other hand, if the water is turbulent or you are about to drown, that could symbolize that you are feeling overwhelmed by your emotions or that there is something in your life that is out of control.

The interesting thing about symbols in dreams is that they don't always have the same meaning for everyone. While there are general interpretations of certain symbols, such as water or animals, each person has their own experience and memories that influence the way symbols appear in dreams. For example, for someone who is afraid of dogs, dreaming about a dog might symbolize fear or anxiety. But for someone who loves dogs, that same dream might represent friendship, loyalty, or protection. So when interpreting symbols in dreams, it's important to take into account our personal emotions and associations.

In addition to objects and animals, actions that occur in dreams can also be symbolic. If you dream that you are running, you might ask yourself: What or who am I running from? The act of running can symbolize that you are trying to escape from something in your life, whether it be a problem, a responsibility, or even an emotion that you don't want to face. Instead, if in the dream you are running freely and enjoying the feeling, it can represent that you feel in control and capable of overcoming obstacles that come your way. This is where the context of the dream becomes essential to correctly interpreting the symbol.

Another fascinating aspect of dreams is that the places that appear in them can also have symbolic meaning. Dreaming about a house, for example, is often related to your own self or mind. Different rooms in the house can represent different aspects of your life. If you dream that you are in the basement, this could symbolize that there are deep emotions or thoughts that you have been holding in and have not yet processed. If you find yourself in the kitchen, perhaps the dream is related to nourishment, both physical and emotional. Each part of the house can have a symbolic meaning related to your inner life.

Even the people in your dreams can be symbols. Sometimes we dream about people we know, but those people may not literally represent who we see, but rather aspects of ourselves. For example, if you dream about a close friend who is very brave, perhaps the dream is trying to tell you that you need to connect more with that brave part of yourself. Other times, people in dreams can represent qualities we admire or fear. So the next time you dream about someone, think not only about that person, but also about what they represent to you.

Dreams can also contain symbols that refer to past events or future decisions we need to make. For example, if you dream of a forked road, this can symbolize a choice you need to make in your life. Perhaps you are facing an important decision and your subconscious is visualizing the different options in the form of paths. In this case, it is important to observe how you feel in the dream. If you feel anxious when choosing one of the paths, perhaps that option is causing you stress in real life. If, instead, you feel relief when taking a direction, it can be a sign that that is the option that will make you feel most at peace.

Not all symbols in dreams are easy to interpret. Some are more personal and may relate to specific memories or experiences. For example, a person who lived near a river as a child and has many happy memories of that place may dream of a river as a symbol of nostalgia or joy. Another person, who may have had a negative experience around water, may interpret a dream about a river in a completely different way. Therefore, a key part of symbolic dream interpretation is reflecting on your own experiences and emotions to understand what each symbol represents for you.

It is important to remember that dreams do not follow the rules of the real world. In a dream, you may see symbols that seem contradictory or impossible. For example, you might dream of an object that is on fire, but at the same time is completely frozen. These types of surreal images often reflect internal conflicts or contradictory emotions that you are experiencing. Although these symbols can sometimes be disconcerting, they are a way for your mind to try to express something complex in a way that cannot always be done directly.

Throughout history, different cultures have used the symbolic interpretation of dreams as a tool to understand the world and make decisions. In many ancient societies, dreams were considered divine messages or premonitions about the future. Although today we understand dreams from a more psychological perspective, the idea that dreams contain important messages still holds true. Symbols in dreams tell us about our emotions, our deepest desires, and our fears, and by paying attention to them, we can learn a lot about ourselves.

The key to interpreting symbols in dreams is to keep an open mind and be willing to explore what those symbols mean to you personally. It's not always easy to figure out a dream right away. Sometimes a symbol may seem completely disconnected from your life in the moment, but over time, its meaning becomes clearer. It can also be helpful to keep a dream journal to jot down symbols that appear frequently. By writing about them and reflecting on their possible meaning, you can begin to notice patterns and discover what your subconscious is trying to communicate to you.

In short, symbols in dreams are like small pieces of a puzzle that, when put together, reveal a bigger picture of your inner life. Through symbolic interpretation, you can explore your emotions, resolve internal conflicts, and better understand what's going on in your mind. Each symbol is an opportunity to learn something new about yourself and how you're navigating the world. So the next time you dream, pay attention to the details, the objects, the people, and the actions, because they can all hold the key to uncovering a deeper message your mind is trying to send you.

Connecting with the Deep

Connecting with the deep is a process that, although it can sometimes seem complicated, is essential to understand the messages that dreams offer us. When we talk about the deep, we refer to those most hidden layers of our mind and our emotions, those places that we do not always access consciously in daily life. Dreams are a window to that inner world, but to take advantage of them, we need to learn to listen to what they tell us and interpret what they really mean.

In our daily lives, our minds are busy with many things: responsibilities, tasks, worries, and distractions. All of this can cause us to lose touch with what we really feel or think. However, when we sleep, our conscious mind relaxes, and that's when the subconscious, that deeper part of ourselves, starts to communicate. Dreams are a kind of bridge between our conscious self and our deeper mind, a place where our emotions, desires, fears, and experiences intertwine.

Connecting with the deep through dreams involves being willing to explore those messages that may seem confusing or even uncomfortable. Many times, our dreams show us aspects of our lives that we prefer to avoid or that we haven't had the time to properly process. Maybe there is an unresolved conflict, a repressed emotion, or a desire that we haven't recognized. Dreams invite us to pay attention to those areas of our lives that need to be explored so that we can grow and move forward.

A key aspect of connecting with the deep is attention to detail. Dreams can often seem chaotic or messy, but each element has potential meaning. The colors, objects, people that appear, and emotions we feel in dreams are all clues that help us unravel their meaning. For example, if you dream that you are in a place you know, but everything is dark or out of place, this could symbolize that you are feeling confused or lost in some aspect of your life. Maybe there is something that is not working out the way you expected and your subconscious is trying to alert you to it.

It's important to remember that we don't always understand a dream at the moment we have it. Sometimes the meaning of a dream can take days or even weeks to fully reveal itself. This doesn't mean that the dream isn't valuable. In fact, it's part of the process of connecting with the deep, where the puzzle pieces fall into place as you give yourself time to reflect on what you saw. Keeping a dream journal can be a great way to delve deeper into this process, as it allows you to record your dreams and revisit them over time to notice recurring patterns or themes.

Another aspect of connecting with the deep is the willingness to face the unknown. Dreams can take us to unexpected places, show us situations we don't fully understand, or even scare us. But rather than ignoring these dreams or dismissing them as mere fantasies, we can see them as opportunities to better understand our deeper emotions. Perhaps a dream about a sudden fall symbolizes a fear of failure or a sense of loss of control in your life. By being willing to explore those emotions, you open the door to a deeper understanding of yourself.

In addition, dreams can offer you a clearer view of your desires and aspirations, even those you have not consciously acknowledged. Sometimes, we dream about what we really want, but for some reason we do not allow ourselves to desire in daily life. You may dream about a new career, a relationship, or a project that you have not seriously considered, but that deep down is something you long for. Dreams give you the opportunity to explore those desires without the limitations that you sometimes impose on yourself during the day. In this sense, connecting with the deep through dreams can help you discover what you really want in life.

It's important to mention that this connection to the deep isn't just about interpreting dreams from an intellectual perspective. Sometimes, what dreams reveal to us is something we feel rather than something we understand. The emotions we experience in dreams are a direct reflection of what's going on inside us. If you feel at peace in a dream, that can be a sign that you're aligned with your true desires and emotions. If, instead, you feel anxious or restless, perhaps there's something you haven't yet processed or that you need to address in your waking life.

Connecting with the deep can also help with healing. Through dreams, our minds have the opportunity to process painful or difficult experiences. Many people have experienced dreams where they relive situations from the past, and while this can sometimes be upsetting, it is also an opportunity to release those trapped emotions. Dreaming about a conversation you never had or a situation you were never able to resolve in real life can be a way your mind is trying to find closure or healing. These dreams can be powerful, and while they may not offer a direct solution, they are a way to confront what you have been avoiding.

Connecting with the deep through dreams is not always a linear process. Sometimes you may have a series of dreams that seem completely unrelated, and then suddenly a dream offers you incredible clarity about an aspect of your life. Patience is key in this process. It's not about forcing an immediate interpretation, but rather allowing dreams to guide you toward a greater understanding of yourself over time. By staying open and receptive to the messages from your dreams, you allow yourself to connect with those parts of yourself that may be hidden or unexplored.

Finally, it's important to remember that dreams are just one of many ways we can connect with the depths of our being. Dreams offer us a unique avenue to explore our emotions, desires, and fears, but we can also work on that connection through meditation, reflection, and conscious self-analysis. What's special about dreams is that they allow us to access parts of our mind that we often overlook during the day. They show us what lies beyond the surface and invite us to look beyond the obvious.

Connecting with the deep is an ongoing process. It's not about understanding a specific dream or finding a quick answer. It's more of a way of life, a way of approaching yourself with curiosity, openness, and respect. As you pay attention to your dreams and allow yourself to explore what they're telling you, you may discover aspects of yourself that will surprise you. This connection with the deep will help you not only better understand your dreams, but also navigate life with more clarity, authenticity, and purpose.

Dreams and Emotions

Dreams and emotions are deeply connected. Often when we dream, we are processing emotions that we may not have had the time or space to deal with during the day. Dreams become a kind of outlet for our emotions, whether it be joy, sadness, fear, anger, or confusion. The interesting thing about this process is that we are often unaware of what we are really feeling until we see it reflected in a dream. Emotions in dreams tell us about what is really going on inside us, even if we haven't had the chance to consciously acknowledge it.

Let's think about how a dream can capture an emotion so vividly. Sometimes, you might have a dream that makes you feel incredibly happy, like you're floating on air or laughing non-stop. These types of dreams often reflect a state of satisfaction or fulfillment somewhere in your life. Maybe you feel at peace with your relationships or have found balance in your daily life. What your mind is doing in that dream is projecting that emotion of joy so that you can experience it in a deeper way.

On the other hand, dreams can also reflect more difficult emotions. If you've had a stressful day or have been dealing with a complicated situation, it's quite possible that that tension is showing up in your dreams. Maybe you dream that you're running aimlessly, caught in a storm, or trying to escape from something. These scenarios are metaphors for what you're feeling: the feeling of being overwhelmed, of not being in control, or of trying to escape an uncomfortable situation. Dreams allow you to experience those emotions without restrictions, and while they can sometimes feel disturbing, they're also a way for your mind to try to process what you're experiencing.

The fascinating thing about dreams is that they aren't always a direct representation of our emotions. Sometimes a dream may seem totally disconnected from what we're feeling in daily life, but upon closer inspection, we may discover that it's speaking to a hidden or unexpressed emotion. For example, you might have a dream in which you find yourself lost in an unfamiliar city. At first glance, this might not seem related to what you're experiencing, but upon reflection, you might realize that you're feeling lost or disoriented in some area of your life. Maybe you're having doubts about your career or feeling insecure about a relationship, and your dream is manifesting that confusion in the form of a loss scenario.

Another emotion that frequently appears in dreams is fear. Fear dreams can range from dangerous situations, such as being chased by someone, to more subtle ones, such as the fear of failing or making a fool of yourself. These dreams often arise when we are facing stressful situations or when we feel insecure in some aspect of our life. Sometimes, fear in dreams shows us what we do not want to consciously face, such as the fear of failing in an important project or losing something valuable. Dreaming about these situations is a way to release that fear and face it, even if it is in a fictional scenario.

Emotions are not only expressed through what happens in dreams, but also through the physical sensations we experience in them. We've all had those dreams where we feel an emotion so strong that it seems real: the anguish of a parting, the euphoria of a triumph, or the relief of escaping a dangerous situation. Those physical sensations are a sign that our body is also involved in the process of experiencing and processing emotions while we sleep. Dreams are not just images in our minds, but are complete experiences that include our deepest feelings.

Emotions in dreams aren't always linear. Sometimes a single dream can contain a mix of emotions that seem contradictory. For example, you might dream about a situation that makes you feel happy and, at the same time, anxious. This is because our emotions aren't always simple; we often feel more than one thing at a time. Dreams reflect that emotional complexity, allowing us to explore how different feelings can coexist within us. Maybe in daily life you're excited about a new opportunity, but also afraid of the unknown. In the dream, those emotions are combined and expressed simultaneously, allowing you to process them in a more complete way.

One of the most powerful emotions we experience in dreams is sadness. Dreaming about losing something or someone can be a way our mind tries to deal with pain or grief. Even if we haven't lost someone in real life, we might dream about loss as a metaphor for other things we've left behind: a stage of life, a relationship, an opportunity. These dreams allow us to feel the weight of that sadness and often offer a space to process grief in a way that isn't always possible during the day.

There are also dreams where we experience anger or frustration. Maybe in the dream you are arguing with someone or you are unable to achieve something you set out to do. These dreams can be a sign that there are repressed emotions in your daily life. Sometimes, we do not express our anger or frustration consciously because we do not want to confront the people or situations that generate those emotions. Dreams, however, do not have those limitations. In a dream, you can express all your anger without the social restrictions that you have in real life, and although it may not be pleasant, it is a healthy way to release those accumulated tensions.

Another common emotion in dreams is surprise or confusion. We often dream about situations that seem completely absurd or make no sense to us, and this can create a feeling of bewilderment. These dreams may be reflecting situations in our life where we feel disoriented or out of control. Maybe we are facing an unexpected change or feel out of place in some part of our life, and the dream reflects that feeling through chaotic or disconcerting situations.

But not all dreams are filled with difficult emotions. There are also dreams that bring us comfort, peace, and tranquility. These dreams often appear when we have reached a state of emotional balance or when we are in a healing process. Maybe we dream of serene landscapes, such as a quiet beach or a field full of flowers, and those images bring us a sense of calm. These dreams are a sign that our mind is in a place of rest and that our emotions are in balance.

To better understand our emotions through dreams, it's helpful to pay attention to how we feel when we wake up. Sometimes the content of the dream can be difficult to remember, but the emotions we feel when we wake up are often clear. If you wake up feeling anxious, sad, or relieved, those emotions may be a sign of what your subconscious was processing during the dream. Those feelings can offer clues about what's going on in your emotional life, even if you don't remember all the details of the dream.

In short, dreams are a mirror of our deepest emotions. Through them, we have the opportunity to process what we feel, even when we are not consciously aware of those emotions in our daily lives. Paying attention to how we feel in dreams, and upon awakening, offers us a window into our inner world, helping us to better understand our emotions and find ways to balance them. Dreams, at their core, are a free expression of our emotional being, and by exploring them, we can learn to connect more deeply with what we truly feel.

Dreams as a Reflection of Anxiety

Dreams that reflect anxiety are a very common experience. When we are worried, stressed, or going through difficult times, our dreams often reflect those feelings. Instead of disappearing when we fall asleep, anxiety finds a way to show itself in the dream world, taking different forms and scenarios that can sometimes be confusing or disturbing. However, these dreams are not simply nightmares or negative situations. In fact, they can be a valuable tool to better understand what we are feeling and how we can cope with it.

Imagine that during the day you are faced with a stressful situation: a problem at work, a personal conflict, or worry about the future. Even if you try to distract yourself or carry on with your routine, anxiety builds up in your mind. When you finally go to sleep, that anxiety doesn't magically disappear. On the contrary, your mind continues to process it, and it does so through dreams. Often, these dreams can be a kind of distorted reflection of what worries you in daily life. Instead of dreaming directly about the situation that makes you anxious, you might dream about something symbolic, such as running without being able to reach a destination or getting lost in an unknown place.

One of the most common dreams associated with anxiety is a dream in which you find yourself in a situation in which you have lost control. Perhaps you dream that you are driving a car, but you cannot stop, or that you are running, but you cannot move forward. These dreams often represent the feeling of helplessness that accompanies anxiety. When we are anxious, we often feel like we cannot control what is happening around us, and that is reflected in our dreams in symbolic ways. The mind takes that feeling of lack of control and transforms it into images that are familiar, but disturbing.

Another type of dream that is typical when we are anxious is that of being in risky or dangerous situations. You may dream that someone is chasing you or that you are about to fall from a high place. These dreams are a manifestation of the fear that accompanies anxiety. Many times, the fear of the unknown or of what can go wrong in real life turns into a feeling of impending danger in the dream. Although these dreams can be disturbing, it is important to remember that they are not predictions of what will happen in reality. Instead, they are a representation of how you feel in the face of uncertainty.

It is common for anxiety dreams to also feature exam situations or being faced with a challenge for which you are not prepared. Many people dream that they have to take an exam and have not studied, or that they are in an important presentation without having prepared. These dreams reflect the fear of failure and not living up to expectations, whether from others or from yourself. This type of dream is usually very common at times when you feel insecure or under pressure, such as before a job interview, a real exam, or a difficult conversation.

Dreams that are associated with anxiety may also include a sense of loss. Perhaps you dream that you lose something valuable, such as your keys, your phone, or even a loved one. These dreams may be related to the fear of losing control of some important situation in your life. The mind translates that worry into the image of losing objects or people, which in the dream feels like great frustration or distress. However, what it is really reflecting is your fear of not being able to handle everything at hand.

It's important to note that not all anxiety-related dreams are necessarily negative or scary. Sometimes, dreams can present a more abstract version of what's troubling you. For example, you might dream about an endless maze or about trying to solve a complex problem without finding the solution. These dreams are more symbolic, but they still reflect the feeling of being trapped in anxiety or not finding a clear way out of the difficulties you're facing. In these cases, the dream can be a kind of metaphor for the confusion or mental exhaustion you're feeling.

One of the things that's interesting about dreams and anxiety is that although dreams can seem confusing or even scary, they can actually be useful in helping us deal with our fears and worries. Sometimes dreaming about what scares us is a way to process those emotions. By seeing those worries reflected in a dream, we can become aware of what's really affecting us and begin to work on how to deal with it. Dreams offer us a safe space where our emotions can be expressed without the constraints of the real world.

For example, if you have a dream in which you're being chased by something or someone, you might ask yourself: What am I really avoiding or fearing in my life? The dream isn't just there to scare you; it's trying to show you what you haven't consciously wanted to face. By interpreting the dream in this way, you can begin to break down the anxiety into more manageable parts and think about how you might deal with those emotions in your daily life.

Sometimes anxiety dreams also show us possible solutions or paths to follow. In some dreams, even though you start off feeling anxious or trapped, you might find a way out or a way to resolve the situation. Maybe in the dream you finally manage to escape from what is chasing you or find what you had lost. These dreams can be a sign that even though anxiety is present, you also have the ability to face it and find solutions. In a sense, dreams show us not only our fears, but also our strengths.

Another interesting aspect of anxiety-related dreams is how they connect to the body. Many people report physical sensations while dreaming, such as a racing heart or a feeling of being paralyzed. This is because anxiety not only affects our mind, but also our body. Even while we sleep, our body can react to the emotions we are processing in the dream. This is why you sometimes wake up from an anxiety dream feeling like you just ran a marathon or feeling like you've been trapped in a real physical situation.

One way to approach these dreams is to take the time to reflect on them once you wake up. Instead of dismissing them as just nightmares, ask yourself what they were showing you about your anxiety. Is there something in your daily life that you're not dealing with? Is there a worry that's been lingering in your mind without you realizing it? Sometimes, just acknowledging that you're anxious can help relieve some of that internal pressure. Dreams can act as a mirror for your emotions, and the more you understand them, the better you'll be able to handle what's affecting you.

It's also helpful to remember that dreams aren't prophecies. An anxiety dream doesn't mean that what you're dreaming about will happen in real life. For example, if you dream that you're losing someone, it doesn't mean that person will disappear. Instead, that dream is more likely speaking to your own inner fears, not a literal prediction. Understanding this can be a huge relief, as it allows you to see dreams for what they really are: expressions of your emotions, not warnings about the future.

Finally, it's important to note that anxiety dreams are a normal part of life. We all go through times of stress, and our dreams reflect that. The valuable thing is that by paying attention to them and learning from them, we can discover ways to manage our anxiety more effectively. Dreams can be uncomfortable, but they are also a window into our inner world, and by exploring them, we can find keys to improving our emotional and mental health.

In conclusion, dreams as a reflection of anxiety are a powerful tool for self-knowledge. Although they may be uncomfortable or disturbing, they offer us a clear insight into what is really going on in our minds and hearts. By paying attention to these dreams and reflecting on them, we can learn to deal with anxiety more effectively, discovering not only our fears, but also our strengths.

The Role of Sleep in Problem Solving

Dreams play a fascinating role in problem solving. Although it may not seem like it at first glance, while we sleep our minds continue to work in ways we don't always understand. We often go to bed worried about a situation or challenge, and when we wake up, we may find a new perspective or even a solution we hadn't considered before. This phenomenon, where dreams help us solve problems, is something that has intrigued people for centuries.

During the day, our minds are busy with many tasks: work, family, responsibilities, and everything else that requires our attention. Sometimes when we are faced with a problem, it can seem impossible to find a solution because we are so wrapped up in the stress and hustle and bustle of daily life that we fail to see beyond it. However, when we sleep, our minds are free from these distractions. Instead of being occupied with the demands of everyday life, they are free to explore solutions creatively and without the limitations that reality imposes.

One of the most interesting aspects of sleep is that it allows the brain to reorganize the information it has received during the day. When we try to solve a problem while awake, we are often limited by the thinking patterns we normally use. If we don't find a solution right away, we may feel frustrated or stuck, and that only increases stress. However, when we sleep, our mind enters a state where those barriers are broken down. The brain begins to process information in new ways, making connections that we may not have considered before.

This process is part of what is known as memory consolidation. While we sleep, our mind is not only filing away the day's memories and experiences, but it is also reorganizing that information to make it more accessible. This means that if we have been working on a problem before we fall asleep, our brain is still "working" on it while we sleep, reorganizing the details and looking for new ways to solve it. Sometimes this reorganization leads to what is known as a "lightbulb moment," where we suddenly wake up with a solution we hadn't previously considered.

A classic example of how dreams can help solve problems comes from stories of inventors, scientists, and artists who have found solutions or inspiration while asleep. Perhaps one of the best-known examples is that of German chemist August Kekulé, who dreamed of a snake biting its tail and, upon awakening, realized that the image represented the structure of benzene, a molecule he had been studying. This is just one of many instances where dreams have played a crucial role in solving complex problems.

The reason why dreams are so effective at problem-solving has a lot to do with the way the brain works during sleep. During REM, which is when most vivid dreams occur, the brain is incredibly active. However, the part of the brain that is responsible for logic and critical reasoning, the prefrontal cortex, is less active during sleep. This means that our minds are freer to explore creative ideas and innovative solutions without the constraints of rational thinking that we normally apply when we are awake. In other words, sleep allows our creativity to flow in a way that is much harder to achieve when we are conscious.

This process of problem-solving through dreams isn't always immediate. Sometimes, you might dream about a problem for several nights before you come up with a solution, or maybe dreams simply offer you a new perspective that helps you see the problem from a different angle. What's important, though, is that dreams give you the opportunity to access a more intuitive and creative part of your mind, which often leads to more innovative solutions.

An interesting aspect of dreaming is that we don't always have to directly dream about the problem for the dream to help us solve it. Sometimes dreams can seem completely irrelevant to what we're trying to solve, but upon awakening, we may see that they've given us an insight or a clue that brings us closer to the answer we're looking for. It's as if the dream is working in the background, reorganizing information and making connections we hadn't seen before. Although it's not always apparent at the time, these dreams can be instrumental in finding solutions to everyday life's problems.

It's not just intellectual or work-related problems that can benefit from the process of dreaming. Emotional and personal challenges can also find answers while we sleep. When we're faced with a difficult decision or a complex emotional situation, it's sometimes hard to see clearly what we should do. Anxiety and confusion can cloud our judgment. However, when we sleep, those emotions are processed differently. Perhaps you dream about a symbolic situation that, upon awakening, gives you clarity about how you really feel or what path you should take.

Another way dreams help us solve problems is by allowing us to rehearse different scenarios. Sometimes, when we are facing an important decision, we might dream about different possible outcomes. In these dreams, our mind is exploring the consequences of our actions in a safe way, without us having to take risks in real life. For example, if you are trying to decide between two options, you might dream about the possible consequences of both and, upon waking, feel more confident about which is the best choice.

The process of problem-solving through sleep can also be very helpful when we find ourselves in situations where we need to think strategically or creatively. For example, if you are working on a project that requires new ideas, sometimes sleep can offer you unexpected inspiration. You may wake up with a brilliant idea or a different approach that you had not considered before. This is particularly true in the artistic field, where dreams often act as a source of creativity. Painters, writers, musicians, and filmmakers often find ideas in their dreams that they then transform into works of art.

To harness the power of dreams in problem solving, it's helpful to pay attention to what you dream about and keep a record of your dreams. Keeping a dream journal is a great way to capture those ideas and moments of inspiration that may come to you while you're sleeping. Sometimes dreams can seem confusing or nonsensical at first, but by writing them down and reflecting on them, you may discover important details or patterns that help you work through what you're facing in your daily life.

Another helpful trick is to think about the problem right before you go to sleep. If you have something on your mind that you can't figure out how to solve, simply meditate on it for a few minutes before you close your eyes. This sends a signal to your subconscious that it's something you're working on, and can increase the likelihood that you'll dream up a solution or a new perspective. This method, known as "dream incubation," has been used by many people throughout history to solve problems of all kinds, from scientific challenges to emotional dilemmas.

In short, dreams aren't just a way to rest. They're also a powerful tool for problem-solving, both big and small. While we sleep, our minds continue to work in the background, processing the day's information and searching for new ways to solve the challenges we face. By paying attention to our dreams and using their ability to generate new ideas, we can discover innovative solutions that we might not have found while awake. Dreams, at their core, are a fundamental part of the human thought process, a window into our creativity and our unique problem-solving ability.

Myth or Reality?

Throughout history, dreams have been the focus of myths, legends and beliefs. From ancient civilizations to the present day, many cultures have tried to decipher their meaning, wondering whether dreams are simply a product of the mind, without any relevance, or whether they actually have a deeper value that can guide us in our daily lives. This dilemma of whether dreams are myth or reality has been a subject of fascination for centuries, and still makes us wonder today: are they just meaningless illusions or do they have a real meaning?

On the one hand, there is the view of dreams as simple creations of the brain, an activity without much purpose beyond processing what we experience during the day. This perspective, heavily influenced by modern science, holds that dreams are just the result of brain activity while we sleep, a natural process that occurs while our brain is still working. According to this view, dreams are nothing more than a mixture of memories, emotions and fragments of experiences that are randomly combined, and any attempt to interpret them would be in vain, since they have no meaning beyond what we see in them.

However, this explanation is not enough for many people. Throughout history, there have been countless examples of dreams that seem to have predicted future events or that have had a profound impact on the lives of those who have experienced them. We often hear stories of people who dream about something that later happens in reality, or who find in their dreams an answer or a sign that guides them in their decisions. These experiences have led many to believe that dreams are more than just images produced by the brain; that they actually contain messages or clues that can help us understand what is happening in our lives.

Ancient civilizations, such as the Egyptians, Greeks, and Romans, strongly believed that dreams were messages from the gods. To them, dreams had sacred meaning and could be a form of divine communication. Priests and oracles interpreted dreams to predict the future or to guide leaders in their decisions. In these cultures, dreaming was not just an everyday phenomenon, but a way to receive wisdom and guidance. They believed that through dreams, the gods could warn humans about impending dangers or show them the right path to follow. These beliefs endured for centuries, and to this day, in many cultures, dreams are still seen as more than just meaningless images.

In contrast, other cultures and philosophies viewed dreams as a window into the subconscious. Sigmund Freud, one of the fathers of modern psychology, proposed that dreams are an expression of our deepest desires, those that we often fail to recognize while awake. According to Freud, dreams are not divine messages, but they do have hidden meanings that reflect our inner conflicts and repressed desires. For him, every image and symbol in a dream had a meaning that could help us better understand our mind and emotions. This view of dreams as a manifestation of the unconscious has been highly influential in the field of psychology, and many still believe that dreams can offer us clues about what we truly feel or desire, even if we are not fully aware of it.

In this context, the question arises: if dreams reflect our deepest thoughts and emotions, are they then a form of reality? While the events we experience in dreams do not occur in the physical world, the emotions and sensations we feel while dreaming can be very real. Sometimes a dream can be so vivid that upon awakening we are left with a strong impression of what we have experienced. We may feel sad, happy, scared or confused by what we have dreamed, showing that even though dreams may not be "real" in the physical sense, they do have a genuine emotional impact on our lives.

Another common belief is that dreams can be premonitory in nature, meaning they can anticipate or warn us about future events. Throughout history, there are many accounts of people who claim to have dreamed about an event before it happened. Some consider these dreams to be mere coincidences, but others believe there is something more at play, such as a mysterious connection between the dream world and the future. Although science has not been able to prove that dreams can predict the future, these experiences remain a source of intrigue for many.

The truth is that, despite all the scientific advances, dreams remain a mystery in many ways. Science has managed to explain much of the sleep process, from the phases of sleep to how the brain activates during REM sleep, but there is still much we do not fully understand. Dreams touch on a part of our human experience that seems beyond logic and reason. They connect us to our deepest emotions, to our fears, desires and hopes, and sometimes even to aspects of ourselves that we do not recognize while we are awake.

So, are dreams myth or reality? Ultimately, the answer to this question depends on how we choose to view them. If we view them simply as meaningless brain activity, we might think they are just myths, an illusion created by our mind while we sleep. But if we believe that dreams offer us a window into our subconscious, a way to process our emotions, or even a way to receive important messages about our life, then dreams become a powerful reality, a tool we can use to better understand ourselves and the world around us.

Dreams, with their mix of mystery, symbolism and emotion, occupy a unique space between the real and the imaginary. They are a bridge between our conscious life and our deepest thoughts, and although we cannot touch them or see them with our open eyes, their influence on our lives is undeniable. Through dreams, we explore unknown territories of our mind, confront fears, find answers and sometimes discover aspects of ourselves that we had not recognized before.

So, while we cannot definitively answer whether dreams are myth or reality, what is clear is that they have immense power to influence our lives, whether on an emotional, psychological or even spiritual level. Dreams are a space where the impossible becomes possible, and where the barriers of logic are broken to make way for a deeply human experience, an experience that, regardless of whether it is real or not, has the power to change the way we see the world and understand ourselves.

Lucid Dreams

Lucid dreams are one of the most fascinating phenomena in the world of dreams. They are those moments when, while we are dreaming, we realize that we are dreaming. Instead of being mere spectators of what is happening, we can take control of our actions and the direction that the dream takes. It is as if we were inside a movie, but this time we are the directors, the protagonists and the scriptwriters at the same time.

Imagine that you are dreaming that you are flying over a city. Suddenly, something in your mind tells you that what is happening is not real, that you are in a dream. At that moment, you realize that you can control what is happening. You can fly higher, change the scenery, or even decide to do things that would be impossible in real life. This type of experience is what we call a lucid dream, and the feeling of power is truly impressive.

Unlike normal dreams, where we simply go with the flow of the situations our mind presents to us, in a lucid dream we are aware that we are dreaming. This awareness gives us incredible freedom to explore whatever we want. We can face our fears, try out new skills, or simply enjoy the experience of flying, traveling to imaginary worlds, or talking to people who are not present in our everyday lives.

But how is it possible for us to have this experience? How can someone realize they are dreaming while still in a dream? Science has studied lucid dreaming for many years, and while there is still much we don't understand, we do know that it occurs when the part of the brain responsible for logic and decision-making is partially activated during sleep. This allows us to maintain some level of consciousness while we are still asleep, allowing us to recognize that what is happening is not real.

One of the most interesting features of lucid dreaming is that it doesn't just happen spontaneously. With some practice, it's possible to train our minds to have more lucid dreams. Many people who have mastered this skill use specific techniques to notice that they are dreaming. For example, one common technique is to perform "reality checks" during the day. These tests involve constantly asking ourselves whether or not we are dreaming. By doing this frequently while we are awake, we gradually begin to do it in our dreams as well, and this helps us recognize when we are dreaming.

Another technique for inducing lucid dreaming is the use of so-called "conscious awakenings." This involves waking up in the middle of the night, staying awake for a few minutes, and then going back to sleep with the intention of having a lucid dream. By doing so, you are more likely to enter the REM phase of sleep, which is when most lucid dreams occur, with a higher level of consciousness. These techniques may take some practice, but many people have been able to have frequent lucid dreams using these methods.

So why would we want to have lucid dreams? There are many reasons why people enjoy this experience. One of the most obvious is fun. In a lucid dream, we can do things that would be impossible in real life, such as flying, walking through walls, or having superpowers. For many people, the feeling of freedom and control experienced in a lucid dream is incredibly exciting.

However, lucid dreaming is not just a source of entertainment. It can also be a powerful tool for personal growth and problem solving. Some people use lucid dreaming to confront their fears and phobias. For example, if someone is afraid of heights, they may dream that they are in a height situation and confront it in a safe environment, knowing that it is only a dream. By doing this repeatedly, they may find that their real-life fear diminishes.

Additionally, lucid dreaming can also be used to explore emotional or personal issues. In a lucid dream, we may have conversations with characters who represent aspects of our own mind or emotions. By talking to these "people" in the dream, we may discover things about ourselves that we had not recognized while awake. Some people even claim to have found answers to important questions about their lives or solved complex problems while in a lucid dream.

Another advantage of lucid dreaming is that it can be a tool to improve our skills. For example, athletes or musicians can use lucid dreaming to practice their skills in a mental setting. Even though they are not actually performing the actions in the physical world, the intense visualization in the lucid dream can help improve performance in real life. This is because in many cases, the brain does not fully distinguish between a real action and an action visualized in great detail. Therefore, practicing in a lucid dream can be an effective way to hone our skills.

For many people, lucid dreaming is also an opportunity to explore their creativity. Artists, writers, and creators of all kinds have used lucid dreaming as a source of inspiration. In a lucid dream, the rules of reality don't apply, meaning we can create imaginary worlds, unique characters, and unlikely situations. This creative freedom can lead us to new ideas and concepts that we would never have considered in our waking life.

However, not everyone has the same facility for experiencing lucid dreaming. For some people, lucid dreaming comes naturally and frequently, while for others it is more rare and difficult to achieve. This does not mean that it is impossible to have lucid dreams if you have not experienced them before. With some practice and patience, it is possible to increase the frequency of lucid dreaming and even learn to have them on a regular basis.

Despite all the advantages of lucid dreaming, it is also important to remember that it is not completely controllable. Although we can influence what happens in a lucid dream, we cannot always control every aspect of the dream. Sometimes, dreams can take unexpected turns or become more intense than we would like. This is part of the nature of dreams, that although we can influence them, they are still largely a product of our unconscious mind.

For those who wish to experience lucid dreaming, it is helpful to keep a dream journal. Writing down our dreams upon waking can help us remember more details and recognize patterns in them. The more aware we are of our dreams, the easier it will be to recognize when we are dreaming and take control of the dream. Additionally, the simple act of paying attention to our dreams can make our minds focus more on them, increasing the likelihood of having a lucid dream.

In short, lucid dreaming is an extraordinary experience that allows us to explore our minds in a unique way. It gives us the opportunity to take control of our dreams, face our fears, practice skills, and explore our creativity without the limitations of the physical world. Although they are not always easy to achieve, with practice and dedication, many people can experience the incredible feeling of knowing they are dreaming and enjoy the freedom that it offers. Lucid dreaming, at its core, is a window into a world of infinite possibilities, where the impossible becomes possible and where our imagination has no limits.

The Meaning of Colors and Places in Dreams

The colors and places that appear in our dreams often have deeper meanings than we might imagine. Although at first glance they might seem like simple details of the dreamscape, the truth is that these elements can be connected to our emotions, thoughts, and experiences. Colors and places in dreams are not just decorations; they are symbols that our mind uses to communicate with us in subtle and sometimes surprising ways. Understanding what they represent can give us important clues about what is happening in our inner world and about the messages our unconscious is trying to send us.

Let's start with colors. In everyday life, colors often have clear associations and cultural meanings, and dreams are no different. Our minds use colors to express emotions and moods, so paying attention to the colors we see in dreams can help us decipher what we're feeling, even when we're not fully aware of it.

For example, the color red in a dream is often associated with intense emotions such as passion, anger, or danger. If you dream about something or someone that is surrounded by red, it may be a sign that you are experiencing strong feelings in your daily life. Red can be a warning that there is something you need to face or an indication that you are dealing with emotions that have been hidden. On the other hand, red can also represent vitality and energy, depending on the context of the dream.

The color blue, on the other hand, tends to be linked to calmness, tranquility, and inner peace. Dreaming of a clear blue sky or a deep blue sea can be a sign that you are in a serene state of mind, or that you need more calm in your life. Blue can also be linked to introspection, suggesting that the dream may be inviting you to reflect on your emotions and thoughts more deeply. However, in some contexts, blue can represent sadness or melancholy, especially if it appears in dark tones.

The color green is often associated with nature, growth, and renewal. In dreams, seeing the color green can be a sign that you are in a process of personal transformation or that you need to connect more with your natural surroundings. Green can also symbolize health and well-being, which can be an indication that your body or mind is seeking balance. However, green can also have negative connotations, such as envy, especially if it appears disproportionately or in a tense context.

Yellow is a color that is generally associated with joy, energy, and creativity. Dreaming about the color yellow can be a sign that you are feeling optimistic or that you are experiencing a moment of mental clarity. Yellow can also be related to intellect and wisdom, suggesting that you are looking for solutions to problems or exploring new ideas. However, in some cases, yellow can symbolize warnings or cautionary situations, as it is also a color associated with danger signs in real life.

Black and white, although they seem like opposites, both have deep meanings in dreams. Black is often associated with the unknown, the hidden, or the mysterious. If you dream of places or people shrouded in darkness, it may be a sign that there is something in your life that is causing you uncertainty or that you need to explore areas of your mind that you have been avoiding. On the other hand, white is linked with purity, peace, and simplicity. Dreaming of white spaces or white objects may be a sign that you are seeking clarity or that you need to eliminate distractions and focus on the essentials.

Colors in dreams can also change depending on how you feel in the dream. For example, a landscape that would be green and beautiful in real life might appear in gray and dull tones if you are going through a period of sadness or stress. The way we perceive colors in dreams is closely linked to our emotions and moods, making them a powerful tool for understanding what is going on inside us.

Moving on to places, it is important to recognize that the settings where our dreams take place also have symbolic meanings. Like colors, the places we visit in dreams often reflect aspects of our emotional, psychological, or spiritual lives. Sometimes places in dreams are literal representations of places we know, but other times they are completely made up or distorted. The important thing is that whatever the place, it has a purpose and meaning in the narrative of our dream.

A home, for example, often represents our security, our identity, and our deepest emotions. Dreaming about being at home, whether it's your current home or a childhood home, can be a sign that you're dealing with important personal issues. If the house is in good shape, it can be a reflection that you feel balanced and secure. But if the house is in disrepair, it can be an indication that there are areas of your emotional or personal life that need attention.

Dreams that occur in a school or classroom often have to do with learning and personal growth. Dreaming that you are in a classroom can be a sign that you feel like you are learning an important lesson in your life, or that you are facing challenges that require you to acquire new skills or knowledge. It can also be related to feelings of insecurity or fear of failure, especially if in the dream you feel anxious or lost at school.

Natural landscapes, such as mountains, forests, or beaches, also have powerful meanings in dreams. Mountains often symbolize challenges or goals that you are trying to achieve. If you dream about climbing a mountain, it can be a sign that you are working to overcome major obstacles in your life. On the other hand, forests often represent the unknown or the mysterious. Getting lost in a forest can be a sign that you are feeling confused or lost in your life, while walking quietly through a forest can symbolize a desire for connection with your inner nature.

Beaches, with their mix of land and water, are often symbolic of the transition between the conscious and the unconscious. Dreaming about being on the beach can be a sign that you are exploring your emotions or that you need some time to relax and reflect. The sea itself often represents the unconscious, so dreaming about the ocean can be an indication that you are dealing with deep emotions or aspects of your life that are beyond your conscious control.

Cities in dreams are often related to social life and interactions with others. Dreaming about being in a bustling city can be a sign that you are feeling overwhelmed by social demands or the amount of activities you have in your life. On the other hand, an empty or desolate city can be a reflection of the loneliness or isolation you are experiencing. The way you feel in the city in your dream can say a lot about how you perceive your social life or personal relationships.

Even the most abstract buildings or spaces in dreams, such as churches, hospitals, or shopping malls, have their own symbolic meaning. Churches are often related to spirituality and the search for deeper answers, while hospitals can symbolize healing, whether physical or emotional. Shopping malls, on the other hand, are often related to the decisions and choices you need to make in your life.

In short, the colors and places in our dreams are much more than just details. They are powerful tools that our mind uses to express emotions, thoughts, and situations that we may not be able to consciously confront. By paying attention to these elements and reflecting on their meaning, we can gain greater insight into what is going on inside us and use that information to improve our daily lives. Dreams speak to us in a symbolic language, and by deciphering it, we can access a rich source of knowledge about ourselves.

Rebirth and Change

The concept of rebirth and change in dreams is something that many people experience without realizing its true meaning. Dreams related to rebirth often reflect internal processes of transformation, moments when we leave a part of ourselves behind to make way for a new, stronger or wiser version. These types of dreams often occur at times of great change in life, whether when we are facing difficulties or when we are preparing for a new stage. What we dream about can be a way for our mind to show us that we are ready to grow and evolve.

Dreaming about rebirth doesn't always literally mean being born again, although sometimes the imagery in dreams can be quite graphic. It can manifest in a number of different ways: from the feeling that we are starting over in some area of our life, to symbolic images such as flowers blooming, butterflies emerging from their cocoon, or even disasters giving way to something new and better. These symbols reflect the process of personal transformation, a journey we all take at some point.

When we dream about rebirth, it may be that our subconscious is telling us that we are ready to let go of the past. Sometimes, these dreams appear after times of grief, loss, or major changes in our lives. In those cases, dreams help us process what we have left behind, whether it is a relationship, a job, or even a part of ourselves that no longer serves us. Dreams of rebirth are a sign that we are moving into a new stage of our life, one in which we are more aware of what we want and what we need.

Change, meanwhile, is another recurring theme in dreams. Many times, the changes we see in dreams are reflections of the changes we are experiencing in our daily lives, although we are not always aware of them. Dreaming about moving, traveling, or physical transformations can be a way for our mind to show us that we are ready to adapt to new situations. Change is a constant in life, and our dreams help us process it, sometimes preparing us for what is to come.

One of the most interesting aspects of dreams about change is how we feel during the dream. Some people experience these dreams with a sense of fear or anxiety, which is completely normal. Change can be scary, even when we know it's necessary or inevitable. However, our dreams often reveal to us that behind that fear is an opportunity for growth and improvement. If we dream that we're going through a storm or a desert, for example, it can be a sign that we're dealing with challenges, but also that we have the strength to overcome them.

On the other hand, some dreams about change can bring a sense of excitement and anticipation. Dreaming about flying, exploring new places, or discovering something unknown can be a sign that we are open to new experiences and ready to embrace change. These dreams remind us that change doesn't always have to be feared; it can be an adventure that leads us to discover new parts of ourselves. Even when things seem uncertain or out of control, our dreams remind us that change is an opportunity to reinvent ourselves and to find new ways to be happy.

Another key aspect of dreams about rebirth and change is the symbolism of the cycle of life. In many cultures and traditions, the cycle of death and rebirth is a recurring theme, reflecting the belief that everything in life is cyclical. In dreams, this cycle can manifest itself in many ways. For example, dreaming about death is not always a bad omen; in fact, in many cases, it is a symbol of transformation. Death in dreams often represents the end of a stage, a sign that something in our life has come to an end to make way for something new. In this sense, death is just one phase of the natural cycle, and rebirth is the next stage.

Dreams about change can also include natural symbols that represent renewal and growth, such as water. Dreaming about rivers, oceans, or rain is often linked to emotional change. Water is a symbol of purification, cleansing, and new beginnings. If we dream that we are sailing down a river, it can be a sign that we are going with the flow of the changes in our life, while dreaming about a flood can indicate that we feel like the changes are overwhelming us. However, after the storm always comes the calm, and these dreams often end with a sense of relief or resolution.

A clear example of how dreams of rebirth and change can impact our everyday lives is when we dream about leaving behind an old house or familiar place to move to something new. This can symbolize that we are ready to move forward, to leave behind what is known and explore new opportunities. Sometimes, these dreams can bring about some nostalgia or resistance, especially if we are clinging to what we know. However, they can also be a sign that it is time to close one chapter and start another.

In addition to the symbols we mentioned, animals also play an important role in dreams of rebirth and change. Dreaming of animals transforming, such as a snake shedding its skin, can be a symbol that we are leaving an old version of ourselves behind. Animals in dreams often represent our own characteristics or qualities, and seeing an animal undergo a transformation can be a way for our subconscious to show us that we are also changing, adapting, and growing.

Ultimately, dreams about rebirth and change invite us to reflect on the stages of our lives, on what we are leaving behind, and on what we are creating in the present. These dreams offer us a clear vision of our personal evolution process, showing us that change is something natural and necessary. They remind us that, although change can be uncomfortable or challenging, it is also an opportunity to start over, to grow, and to become the best version of ourselves.

By paying attention to the details of these dreams, whether it be the symbols of death and rebirth, changes in the environment, or the feelings we experience during the dream, we can gain greater insight into the changes that are occurring in our daily lives. Dreams provide us with a window into our subconscious, and by interpreting these dreams of rebirth and change, we can find the wisdom and strength we need to face any challenges life throws at us.

The Message of Recurring Dreams

Recurring dreams are those that repeat themselves over and over again throughout our lives, sometimes with slight variations, but with a similar essence. These dreams can be disconcerting, as it seems that our subconscious is trying to send us a message that we cannot decipher. The reality is that recurring dreams are usually related to unresolved problems or situations in our daily lives, and for this reason, they keep appearing until we finally face what they want to show us.

One of the most interesting aspects of recurring dreams is that they are often loaded with powerful symbols. Many people experience dreams where they feel trapped, persecuted, or unable to accomplish a task. These themes are common because they reflect feelings of anxiety, stress, or even fear of facing certain aspects of life. For example, someone who repeatedly dreams about being lost in an unfamiliar city might be experiencing insecurities or a lack of control in their daily life. The mind, instead of consciously resolving these feelings, presents them in the form of repetitive dreams to draw our attention to what we are avoiding.

Another reason why dreams recur is because they are trying to teach us something about ourselves. Recurring dreams often appear when we are in a stage of stagnation or conflict, whether it be emotional, personal, or even work-related. Imagine that you have a dream in which you are running around without getting anywhere. This type of dream can be a representation of how you feel in real life, stuck in a rut or facing obstacles that seem insurmountable. The dream keeps appearing because you are not addressing the problem in everyday life, and your subconscious is trying to give you clues as to what is going on.

It's important to remember that recurring dreams don't have a single, universal interpretation. Although some symbols may be similar among different people, the context of each person's life plays a crucial role in the meaning of the dream. So, if you have a recurring dream, it's helpful to reflect on your current life and ask yourself what aspects you're not addressing. Maybe there's a relationship that needs healing, a decision you're having trouble making, or a fear you need to face. The fact that the same dream keeps coming back is a sign that the message hasn't yet been understood or that the situation that generated it hasn't been resolved.

Recurring dreams can also be a way for our minds to invite us to change. Sometimes people repeatedly dream about the same place or situation until they manage to do something different in the dream. For example, someone who dreams about being trapped in a house may eventually find a way out or discover a new room. This type of evolution in dreams can symbolize that we are making progress in our real life, even if we are not always aware of it. It is as if our minds are telling us that we are ready to change or that we have finally found the answer to what has been bothering us.

Furthermore, recurring dreams are often connected to intense emotions. The emotions we feel during these dreams, whether it be fear, frustration, sadness, or even relief, are an important key to understanding their meaning. If a recurring dream always leaves you with a feeling of anxiety, it may be a sign that there is something in your life that you need to face but have been avoiding. Conversely, if a recurring dream leaves you with a sense of peace or resolution, it could indicate that you have begun to make peace with some aspect of your life.

As we go through our lives, recurring dreams may change or even disappear once we have resolved the situation that was causing them. This is what makes dreams such a valuable tool for self-knowledge. By paying attention to the themes and patterns that recur in our dreams, we can gain a clearer view of what we need to change or address in our daily lives. It's as if our mind uses recurring dreams as a way of telling us, "This is important. Pay attention."

Some people find it helpful to write down their recurring dreams in a journal so they can see patterns or changes over time. By doing so, you may find that certain themes emerge when you're going through times of stress or change in your life. For example, if you notice that you always have the same dream when you're making important decisions or facing difficult situations, that dream is likely related to how you handle pressure or fear of failure. This type of self-observation can help you become more aware of your emotions and deal with them more effectively.

It's also interesting to note that recurring dreams aren't always negative or distressing. Some people have recurring dreams that bring them comfort or remind them of happy times. These dreams can be a way for our mind to connect us to positive memories or offer us a sense of stability during difficult times. Repeatedly dreaming about a place or person that makes us feel safe can be a sign that we're seeking emotional support or need to reconnect with something that brings us joy.

On the other hand, there are those who interpret recurring dreams as messages from the unconscious about our deepest goals and desires. In these cases, dreams can serve as an internal compass that guides us toward what we really want in life. If you have a recurring dream in which you are achieving something you long for, such as reaching an important goal or traveling to a place you have always wanted to visit, this dream could be telling you that you are on the right path or that you need to take steps to make that wish a reality.

At the end of the day, recurring dreams are a window into our subconscious, a way for our mind to show us what's going on beneath the surface. By paying attention to these dreams, we can learn more about our worries, our desires, and our fears. And most importantly, we can use that information to make changes in our real lives, to resolve unaddressed issues, and to move toward a state of greater balance and well-being.

Listening to the message of recurring dreams is a way to connect with ourselves in a deeper way. These dreams are not there to disturb or scare us, but to give us clues about what we need to face. If we learn to interpret their meaning and act accordingly, we can release the tensions that cause them and live in a more full and conscious way. Thus, recurring dreams become a powerful tool for self-discovery and personal growth.

The Impact of Dreams on Mental Health

Dreams have a profound impact on our mental health, even though we are often unaware of it. Every night, as we sleep, our minds delve into a world of images, emotions, and experiences that not only affect how we feel when we wake up, but can also influence our overall well-being. Dreams are not just a random nighttime activity, but an important part of our psychological life. Through them, our brain processes emotions, confronts unresolved issues, and finds ways to adapt to the situations we experience.

One of the first effects that dreams can have on our mental health is the way they help us process stress. When we are going through difficult times or are dealing with constant worries, dreams act as a kind of "escape valve." Through the images and situations we experience in our dreams, our mind can reorganize and process the emotions we have accumulated during the day. While dreams may seem confusing or disconnected from reality, they are loaded with emotional meanings that can help us relieve internal tension. In fact, dreaming allows us to unpack repressed emotions, which can help us wake up with a sense of relief or clarity.

Furthermore, dreams also play an important role in regulating our emotions. Throughout the day, we experience a variety of feelings, from joy and love to fear and frustration. During sleep, especially in the REM phase, the brain is responsible for reorganizing those feelings, filtering out what is relevant and helping us better manage our emotions in daily life. Studies have shown that people who experience vivid and complex dreams are often better able to cope with their emotions in a healthy way, as their dreams provide them with a safe space to experience and process what they are feeling.

A clear example of this is when we dream about situations that make us anxious. Many people have had dreams in which they are faced with situations that they find uncomfortable or stressful, such as getting lost, being chased, or being unprepared for an important task. These dreams may seem distressing in the moment, but they are actually serving a vital function. They allow us to confront our fears in a controlled environment, where there are no real consequences. This can help us emotionally prepare to face similar situations in real life, strengthening our ability to manage stress.

However, when dreams become frequent nightmares, the impact on our mental health can be negative. Nightmares are a way for our mind to express fear, anxiety, or unresolved trauma. While we all occasionally have nightmares, when they become recurrent, they can affect our quality of sleep and therefore our mental well-being. People who suffer from frequent nightmares often wake up feeling exhausted or restless, which can lead to a cycle of insomnia and anxiety. It is important to pay attention to these types of dreams and, if necessary, seek help to understand their cause and reduce their frequency.

The impact of dreams on mental health doesn't stop there. Dreams also play a key role in memory consolidation and learning.

During sleep, the brain reviews the information we've acquired during the day, helping us retain knowledge and skills. But beyond that, the process of dreaming also allows us to make sense of our experiences, integrate what we've been through, and gain new perspectives on our lives. This aspect is especially important for our mental health, as it helps us better understand what we're going through and find solutions to the problems we're facing.

Some people find that by paying attention to their dreams, they can gain valuable insight into their emotional states. For example, if a person is going through a period of major change in their life, they may have dreams related to the theme of travel or transition. These dreams may reflect their inner sense of uncertainty or their desire to move forward, providing a window into their deeper feelings. By analyzing dreams, we can discover patterns that help us better understand our worries, desires, and fears, which in turn can contribute to improving our mental health.

Another important aspect to consider is how dreams can act as an emotional refuge in times of difficulty. During periods of stress or sadness, dreams can provide a space where our more complex emotions have a chance to manifest themselves. Sometimes, this occurs in the form of dreams where we find comfort, where we see loved ones we have lost again, or where we manage to overcome difficulties that seem insurmountable in real life. These dreams act as a kind of "internal therapy," allowing our minds to find a sense of peace or resolution, even if only for a few hours.

On the other hand, lack of sleep or disruption of sleep phases can have negative consequences for our mental health. When we don't get enough sleep or when we don't reach the deep phases of sleep, such as REM sleep, our mind doesn't have the chance to properly process the emotions and experiences of the day. This can lead to increased irritability, anxiety, and even depression. Getting a good night's sleep is essential for our mental health, and dreams play a crucial role in that process. By taking care of our sleep quality, we are also taking care of our mind.

It's fascinating to see how dreams can influence our emotional and psychological state over time. Some people, for example, experience a significant shift in their mental well-being after having an enlightening or deeply symbolic dream. These dreams can offer a new perspective or a sense of clarity that we didn't have before. By paying attention to these dream moments, we can find ways to improve our understanding of ourselves and our problems, which can ultimately lead to greater peace of mind.

In short, dreams are not just a curious phenomenon that occurs while we sleep; they have a real and significant impact on our mental health. They help us process emotions, confront our fears, and adapt to life changes. They also provide us with a space for reflection and problem-solving, allowing us to wake up with a clearer and more balanced mind. By learning to listen to what our dreams are telling us, we can improve our relationship with our emotions and our ability to handle the challenges of everyday life. Dreams are ultimately a powerful tool for keeping our mental health in balance, and paying attention to them can be an important step toward emotional well-being.

Collective Dreams

Collective dreams are a fascinating phenomenon that have captured the imagination of people throughout history. Unlike individual dreams, which are personal and specific to each person, collective dreams refer to dream experiences shared by a group of people, either literally or symbolically. These dreams can manifest in various ways, such as in common symbols and themes among people living in the same society, or even in shared dreams that seem to be connected in some way between the dreamers. Although it may seem like a strange concept, collective dreams can offer us deeper insight into how our mind is not only connected to our own experience, but also to the experience of others and the culture in which we live.

One of the most interesting aspects of collective dreams is how they reflect the concerns, desires, and fears of a society as a whole. Throughout history, cultures have experienced similar dream patterns during times of crisis, change, or uncertainty. For example, during times of war, many people report having dreams about disaster, destruction, or loss. These dreams reflect the collective emotional state of a community that is facing a threat or dangerous situation. It's not that people are dreaming exactly the same thing, but the themes are strikingly similar, suggesting that collective dreams are a way of processing shared emotions on a social level.

Furthermore, collective dreams may also be related to a culture's beliefs and myths. Often, societies have stories, symbols, or archetypes that are passed down through generations and that influence people's dreams. These symbols may appear in the dreams of many individuals over time, creating a sort of shared "archive" of images and themes that resonate with a particular culture. For example, in many ancient cultures, people dreamed of gods, spirits, or mythical figures that represented natural or moral forces. These dreams were not only an expression of individual beliefs, but also a way for society as a whole to process its understanding of the world.

The concept of collective dreams has also been explored by psychologists, such as Carl Jung, who spoke of the "collective unconscious." According to Jung, the collective unconscious is a part of our mind that is not individual, but is made up of experiences, memories, and universal symbols shared by all of humanity. In this sense, collective dreams would be a manifestation of this shared unconscious, a window into the deep themes that connect all human beings. Symbols that appear in dreams, such as water, fire, mountains, or animals, often have universal meanings that transcend cultural boundaries, suggesting that, in some way, we are all connected through our dreams.

Although collective dreams may seem like an abstract idea, there are examples in everyday life that show how they work. For example, when a large number of people dream about an important event that has recently occurred, such as a natural disaster or a significant political event, we are seeing an example of how the collective unconscious manifests itself in dreams.

These dreams reflect the shared concern and emotional impact of what is happening in the world. In some ways, collective dreams act as a mirror of the collective mind of a society, showing what is in the hearts and minds of its members.

Another manifestation of collective dreaming is found in spiritual and religious traditions. In many cultures, dreams are not only seen as an individual experience, but as a form of communication with larger forces, whether divine or spiritual. In these contexts, collective dreams are often interpreted as messages or warnings that affect an entire community. For example, in some indigenous cultures, if several members of a tribe dreamed of the arrival of a particular animal, it was interpreted as a sign that something important was going to happen in the community. These dreams were taken seriously and used to guide collective decisions.

In the modern world, collective dreaming can also be seen in situations where people are emotionally connected, such as in family groups or close communities. Sometimes, family members or close friends report having similar or related dreams within the same time period. Although it is not common for two people to dream exactly the same thing, often the themes and symbols in dreams can coincide, indicating an emotional connection between the dreamers. These shared dreams can strengthen the bonds between people and create a sense of unity or common purpose.

The phenomenon of collective dreaming can also extend to popular culture. Through media, film, literature, and art, people are exposed to images and themes that can then appear in their dreams. In this sense, collective dreaming is a reflection of the culture we live in, as our minds take elements of what we see and experience in society and process them during sleep. For example, after watching a popular horror film, many people may dream of similar scenes or emotions, demonstrating how dreams can be influenced by what we share as a society.

Although we don't always notice it, collective dreams have an impact on our daily lives. They remind us that although our dreams are personal and unique, we are also connected to others on a deep level. Collective dreams allow us to see that we are not alone in our worries, desires, or fears; that others, even if they don't share our exact experiences, may be dreaming about similar themes. This connection between our dreams and those of others can give us a sense of belonging and community, knowing that what we experience in our minds at night is not so different from what others experience.

It is also important to remember that collective dreams are not always negative or distressing. Sometimes shared dreams can be experiences of hope, inspiration, or creativity. In times of positive change or renewal, people may dream of symbols of rebirth, growth, or new opportunities. These dreams reflect the collective emotions of optimism and progress, showing that just as we share our fears, we can also share our hope and dreams for a better future.

In short, collective dreams are a powerful display of how our minds are interconnected on a social, cultural, and emotional level. Through them, we process not only our own experiences, but also the concerns and desires of the people around us. Whether manifested in cultural symbols, shared dreams within close groups, or as an expression of the collective unconscious, collective dreams remind us that we are not alone in our dream experiences. By paying attention to these dreams, we can gain greater understanding of our society and ourselves as part of a larger whole.

The Process of Recording and Analyzing Dreams

Recording and analyzing dreams is a powerful tool that allows us to gain insight into our deepest emotions, thoughts, and desires. Although dreams are often quickly forgotten upon awakening, keeping track of them can give us valuable information about our mental and emotional state. This process not only helps us remember what we dreamed, but also find hidden patterns and meanings that might otherwise go unnoticed. In this chapter, we will explore how we can record our dreams and what steps we can take to analyze them effectively.

The first step to recording your dreams is to develop the habit of writing them down as soon as you wake up. Ideally, you should keep a notebook and pen by your bed so that as soon as you wake up, you can jot down what you remember, even if it's just fragments or loose images. It's important to do this as soon as possible, as dream details often fade quickly as time goes on. Don't worry about writing perfectly or in detail—the most important thing is to capture the essence of the dream, the emotions you felt, and any symbols or events that stood out to you.

If you wake up feeling like you don't remember much of the dream, don't be discouraged. Often, starting to write down what little you remember can trigger more memories. Even if you can only remember one emotion or sensation, write it down. Over time, by creating the habit of recording your dreams, you're likely to become more aware of them and begin to remember more details. Some people find that after practicing this technique for a few weeks, their dream memories become clearer and more vivid.

Once you've recorded your dream, the next step is to take a moment to reflect on what you wrote down. What images, people, or situations appeared in the dream? How did you feel during the dream? Dreams are often charged with intense emotions, whether it's fear, joy, sadness, or confusion. It's helpful to pay attention to these emotions, as they are often the key to understanding the message behind the dream. Sometimes, the emotions we experience in dreams reflect feelings we've been repressing or not addressing in our daily lives.

As you record more dreams, you may begin to notice patterns. For example, you might realize that you frequently dream about the same place, the same person, or a particular situation. These patterns are important, as they could be pointing to something that your unconscious mind is trying to communicate to you. Maybe there is a recurring concern in your life that needs to be resolved, or perhaps you are going through a process of change or transformation that your dreams reflect. Identifying these patterns can be the first step toward a greater understanding of yourself and what is happening in your life.

When it comes to analyzing dreams, one of the most useful methods is to explore the symbols that appear in them. Dreams are full of symbols that, although they may seem strange or disconnected, have deep meanings. For example, dreaming about water is often associated with emotions, while dreaming about flying can be related to freedom or the desire to escape a situation. It is important to remember that symbols in dreams do not have a universal meaning; their interpretation can vary from person to person depending on their personal context. Therefore, it is useful to ask yourself: what does this symbol mean to me? What associations do I have with this place, person, or situation in my life?

Another key aspect of dream analysis is paying attention to seemingly insignificant details. Sometimes, what seems like a small detail in a dream can contain an important message. For example, the clothes you wear in a dream, the colors you see, or even the weather can have symbolic meaning. It's helpful to write down all of these details in your dream log, as they might provide additional clues about the dream's message. Sometimes, when you read through your dreams days or weeks after you wrote them down, you may notice things that didn't seem important at the time.

Once you've identified the symbols and patterns in your dreams, you can begin to look for connections to your daily life. Ask yourself: Is there anything in my life that is related to the themes or emotions in this dream? Sometimes dreams are direct reflections of what we're experiencing, such as stress at work or personal conflicts. In other cases, dreams can offer us a new perspective on situations we've been ignoring or not fully understanding. Analyzing dreams gives us the opportunity to see our lives from another angle and to find solutions or paths we may not have considered before.

In addition to analyzing dream symbols and patterns, it is also helpful to pay attention to recurring dreams. If you have a dream that recurs frequently, it is likely that your mind is trying to point out something that needs to be resolved. Recurring dreams are often related to unprocessed emotions or unresolved situations in our lives. By recording and analyzing these dreams on a regular basis, you can begin to identify what aspects of your life might be causing these dreams to recur. Resolving the issues or emotions underlying these recurring dreams can lead to greater mental and emotional clarity.

Another method for analyzing dreams is to use the technique of free association, which involves writing down or thinking about the first thing that comes to mind when you think of a symbol or situation in the dream. This method can help you uncover hidden meanings or connections that you hadn't initially considered. For example, if you dreamed about a house, you might ask yourself: What does a house mean to me? How do I feel about this place? By allowing your mind to flow freely, you may find associations that reveal more about the meaning of the dream.

It's important to remember that not all dreams have a deep or symbolic meaning. Sometimes, dreams simply reflect things we've seen or experienced recently, with no hidden message. However, even in these cases, dreams can offer interesting insight into how our minds process information and emotions. Whether a dream has a deep meaning or not, recording and analyzing it is always an opportunity to learn more about ourselves and our minds.

The process of recording and analyzing your dreams doesn't have to be complicated or overwhelming. The most important thing is to develop the habit of paying attention to your dreams and taking the time to reflect on them. Over time, you may find that your dreams are not only a window into your unconscious mind, but also a valuable tool for personal growth and self-understanding. By exploring what goes on in your mind while you sleep, you can access a part of yourself that you may not have known about, and this can lead to greater clarity and well-being in your everyday life.

Finally, it's important to remember that dream analysis is a personal process. There are no right or wrong answers, and what works for one person may not work for another. The important thing is to be curious and open to what your dreams have to say. Over time, as you get used to recording and analyzing your dreams, you'll likely begin to see them not just as a curious experience, but as a powerful tool for getting to know yourself and improving your emotional well-being.

Integrating Dreams into Everyday Life

Integrating dreams into everyday life may seem complicated at first, but over time, it can become a natural and deeply enriching practice. Dreams are not only experiences that occur while we sleep; they can also influence how we understand and approach our daily reality. When we learn to pay attention to our dreams and extract their meaning, we can use them as a tool for our personal well-being and to better understand our emotions and thoughts.

The first step to integrating dreams into your daily life is to develop the habit of paying attention to them. Often, dreams go unnoticed or are forgotten shortly after you wake up. However, if you make a conscious effort to remember and reflect on them, you will begin to notice their relevance in your daily life. Keeping a dream journal, as we mentioned in the previous chapter, is a great way to start. Writing down your dreams allows you to not only remember them better, but also to review them later to look for patterns, recurring themes, or messages that can be applied to your daily life.

Once you get into the habit of recording your dreams, the next step is to start reflecting on how the themes and emotions you experience in them may be related to what's going on in your waking life. For example, if you've been dreaming about stressful or upsetting situations, it may be a sign that there's something in your daily life that's causing you anxiety or worry. Dreams can act as a mirror, reflecting back our deepest emotions—even those we may not have consciously acknowledged. By reflecting on these emotions and their connection to our daily lives, we can begin to address them more consciously and constructively.

In addition to reflecting on the themes and emotions in your dreams, it's also helpful to pay attention to the symbols and situations that appear in them. Often, dreams contain symbols that may seem puzzling or strange at first glance, but may actually have deep personal meaning. For example, if you repeatedly dream about a particular place, it could be a reflection of a part of your life that needs attention. Likewise, dreaming about certain objects, animals, or people could be related to aspects of yourself or your life that you're trying to better understand. By exploring these symbols and looking for their personal meaning, you may discover new ways to interpret your dreams and apply them to your everyday life.

Another way to integrate dreams into your daily life is to use them as a source of inspiration. Many people have found that their dreams offer them creative ideas or solutions to problems they face in their daily lives. Dreams, not being limited by the logic and rules of the conscious world, can open us up to new ways of thinking and seeing things. If you find yourself in a difficult or stagnant situation in some aspect of your life, paying attention to your dreams might give you a fresh perspective or an idea you hadn't considered. Many times, the solutions we seek in waking life can emerge unexpectedly in the dream world.

One of the most interesting ways to integrate dreams into everyday life is through decision-making. While it's not about relying entirely on dreams to make important decisions, they can offer additional perspective that helps you make more informed decisions. For example, if you dream about a situation in which you feel trapped or uncomfortable, it may be a sign that something in your life is not aligned with your true desires or values. Likewise, if you have a positive, energizing dream related to a decision you're considering, it may be a sign that that choice is in tune with what you truly want. By using your dreams as a complementary tool in decision-making, you can feel more confident and aligned with your true needs and desires.

In addition to making decisions, dreams can also serve as a tool for self-knowledge. As you begin to pay more attention to your dreams and integrate them into your everyday life, you're likely to begin to discover aspects of yourself that you hadn't noticed before. Dreams often reveal hidden desires, fears, worries, and aspects of our personality that we may not recognize in waking life. By exploring these aspects in dreams, you can learn more about who you are and what you really need to feel fulfilled and at peace. This self-knowledge, in turn, can influence how you relate to others, how you manage your emotions, and how you deal with life's challenges.

Another way to integrate dreams into daily life is to use what you learn from them to improve your emotional well-being. Dreams often alert us to unprocessed emotions or situations we've been ignoring. By paying attention to these messages, we can begin to address those emotions in more conscious and healthy ways. For example, if you have recurring dreams of distress or fear, it may be a sign that there's something in your life that needs to be resolved. By addressing these emotions in waking life, you may find relief and a greater sense of well-being. Similarly, positive, comforting dreams can serve as reminders of the things that bring us joy and peace, helping us to cultivate more of those emotions in our daily lives.

Finally, integrating dreams into everyday life can also involve sharing them with others. Although dreams are a very personal experience, sharing them with friends, family, or even in a dream discussion group can be an enriching experience. By talking about our dreams, we not only learn more about ourselves, but we can also receive new perspectives from others. Sometimes, other people may notice details or patterns in our dreams that we hadn't seen ourselves. Additionally, sharing dreams can strengthen our connections with others, as it allows us to open up and be vulnerable in a way that may not be possible in other areas of our lives.

In short, integrating dreams into everyday life is a process that allows us to harness the knowledge and emotions that emerge in the dream world to improve our waking lives. By paying attention to our dreams, reflecting on their meaning, and applying them to our daily decisions and emotions, we can access a greater understanding of ourselves and our environment. Dreams can be an inexhaustible source of wisdom, creativity, and self-knowledge, and by integrating them into our everyday lives, we can live more consciously, fully, and in tune with our true needs and desires. As you practice this integration, you will discover that dreams are not just something that happens while we sleep, but are also a valuable tool to improve our waking life.